Affiliate Marketing Framework

Your Step-By-Step Roadmap to Understanding and Succeeding in
Affiliate Program

By Obinna Kaluorji

COPYRIGHT PAGE

All rights reserved. No part of this book may be republished in any form or by any means, including photocopying, scanning or otherwise without prior written permission to the copyright holder.

Copyright © 2024 Obinna Kaluorji

Table of Contents

DEDICATION 12

ABOUT THE BOOK 13

INTRODUCTION TO AFFILIATE MARKETING 15

Models of Affiliate Marketing 15

Advantages to Affiliate Marketing 17

AFFILIATE MARKETING ECOSYSTEM 18

Affiliate Marketing Ecosystem Key Players 18

How the Ecosystem Works 20

Key Considerations for Success 23

UNEARTHING THE RIGHT AFFILIATE PROGRAMS 25

1. Set Your Goals and Criteria 25

2. Research Affiliate Networks 26

3. Scrutinize Affiliate Programs 28

4. Apply and Get Started 30

5. Keep a Track Record and Optimize 31

6. Build Relationships 32

CHOOSING YOUR AFFILIATE MARKETING NICHE 33

1. Niche Concept Discernment 33

2. Identifying Your Interests and Expertise 34

3. Do Market Research 35

4. Evaluating Profitability 36

5. Analyzing Competition 37

6. Testing and Validation 37

7. Long-Term Considerations 38

BUILD YOUR ONLINE REPUTATION 40

1. Define Your Brand 40

2. Create a Professional Website 41

3. Develop High-Quality Content 42

4. Engage with Your Audience 43

5. Utilize SEO Best Practices 44

6. Use data to make better decisions 45

7. Think Through Whether to Align or Syndicate 46

8. Ensure Compliance and Trust 47

DRIVING TRAFFIC TO YOUR SITE 48

1. SEO (Search Engine Optimization) 48
2. Social Media Marketing 49
3. Email Marketing 50
4. Content Marketing 51
5. Paid Advertising 52
6. Influencer Marketing 52
7. Online Communities and Forums 53
8. Analyze and optimize 54

AFFILIATE EMAIL MARKETING 55

1. Growing Your Email List 55
2. Segmenting Your Email List 56
3. Optimum email campaigns. 57
4. Power Of Email Automation 58
5. Promoting Affiliate Products 59
6. Testing and Optimizing 60

7. Maintaining Compliance and Best Practices 60

8. Forged and Manage Relationships 61

TURNING YOUR VISITORS INTO SALES 62

1. Optimize Your Landing Pages 62

2. Enhance User Experience (UX) 63

3. Applying Social Proof and Trust Signals 64

4. Personalization and targeting 65

5. Create Irresistible Offers 65

6. Leverage high-converting sales funnels 66

7. Implement A/B Testing 67

8. Create and Save Connection 67

9. Track and Measure Performance 68

AFFILIATE MARKETING TRACKING + ANALYTICS 69

1. Setting Up Tracking 69

2. Key Metrics to Track 70

3. Telemetry tracking tools and platforms 71

4. Analyzing Data 72

5. Making Data-Driven Decisions 73

6. Reporting and Communication.. 74

7. Privacy and Compliance 75

SOCIAL PROOF & REVIEWS IN AFFILIATE MARKETING 76

1. Understanding Social Proof 76

2. Gather and showcase Reviews. 77

3. Compelling Testimonials — How to Write Them 78

4. How to Employ Social Media Impressions 79

5. Trust Badges & Certifications 80

6. Creating A Social Proof Strategy 81

7. Addressing Negative Reviews 82

7. Social Proof.. 82

ETHICAL AND COMPLIANT AFFILIATE MARKETING 84

1. Understanding the Compliance Elements................................ 84

2. Affiliate Disclosure 85

3. Circumvent Deceptive Practices 86

4. Data Privacy and Security.. 87

5. Ethical Marketing Practices 88

6. Working with Affiliates 88

7. Legal Considerations 89

8. Learning and Evolution 90

AFFILIATE MARKETING BUSINESS SCALABILITY 91

1. Current Strategies for Optimizing the Studying 91

2. Diversify Traffic Sources 92

3. Nurture Relationships 93

4. Automation And Operational Simplification 94

5. Continue your education 94

6. Enhance Customer Experience 95

7. Scale Content and Outreach 96

8. Be Aware of Scaling And Optimize Your Channels 96

9. Reach out to New Markets & Audience 97

10. Compliance and ethics 98

AFFILIATE MARKETING WITH INFLUENCERS AND PARTNERS 99

1. Finding The Best Influencers & Partners 99

2. Building Strong Relationships 100

3. Creating Effective Consortium Agreements 101

4. The Art (And Skill) Of Managing Collaborations 102

5. Utilizing influencers content 103

6. Success Metrics and Tweak Strategies 104

8. Influencer and Partner Collaborations at Scale 105

9. Reinforced Compliance and Ethical Practices 106

HOW TO MONETIZE BEYOND AFFILIATE LINKS 107

1. Sponsored Content & Advertorials 107

2. Selling Digital Products 108

3. Subscribers: 108

4. Physical Product Sales 109

5. Hosting Events and Webinars 110

6. Licensing and Royalties 111

7 Advertising and Sponsorship 111

8 Affiliate Marketing Programs 112

9 Mentoring and Coaching 112

10. Crowdfunding and Donations 113

11.	Affiliate Marketing Resource and Tools	113
12.	Licensing Your Content	114

14 COMMON MISTAKES TO AVOID WITH AFFILIATE MARKETING 115

1.	Choosing the Wrong Niche	115
2.	Low-Quality Product Promotion	116
3.	Ignoring SEO and Content Quality	117
4.	Ignoring the Target Audience Needs and Preferences	117
5.	Ignoring Everything But Traffic	118
6.	Not Tracking and Measuring Metrics	119
7.	Not Optimizing for Mobile	120
8.	Spamming with Affiliate links	120
9.	Not Building an Email List	121
10.	Relying on One Traffic Source	122
11.	Not Doing Competitor Analysis	122
12.	Failing at Testing and Optimizing	123
13.	Not developing relationships with affiliate managers	124
14.	Setting Vague Or No Goals and Objectives	125

AFFILIATE MARKETING IS THE FUTURE 126

1. A rise in Artificial Intelligence and Automation 126
2. Influencer or Micro-Influencer marketing 127
3. Mobile and Voice Commerce also Widen in its Adoption 128
4. Better Personalization, Customer Experience 129
5. Increased Transparency and Compliance Focus 129
6. Integrating with New Technologies 130
7. Native advertising has been supplanted by the rise of content marketing 131
8. New Market and Platform Expansion 131
9. The state of the Market Before and After Affiliate Networks And Programs 132
10. Social Commerce Integration 133
11. Focus on Data Privacy and Security 133
12. Improved Affiliates Coaching and Improvement 134

OTHER BOOKS BY THE AUTHOR 135

DEDICATION

I would like to dedicate this book to the following persons for the role they played to the existence of this book;

My wife; for all her encouragements and support. For believing in me and helping me to be a better version of myself. For making me know how unique I am and letting me know that all I do is always the best.

My mum; who single handedly trained us (5 boys) and saw us through school after our dad left us at an early age

My siblings; for all their love and encouragements and for their support at on point or the other.

My relatives; for the role they play in my life and for all their encouragements.

About The Book

Affiliate Marketing Framework is a book designed to arm readers with proper knowledge of the nuts and bolts of affiliate marketing and empower them to earn money in affiliate marketing.

The work starts with the very basics of affiliate marketing, explaining how this business model works and introducing the different parties involved—the advertisers, the affiliates, and the affiliate networks.

In this rich book, you will find a step-by-step guide on how to do everything from finding a profitable niche, searching for the right affiliate programs, and creating an authoritative online presence by designing your websites and branding.

It discusses such strategies that result in real value and content that is of value enough to draw an audience and retain it.

The book highlighted the different tactics of driving traffic which include SEO, paid advertising through social media, optimization of landing pages, and the conversion of visitors to sales through improved user experience. The performance metrics are tracked and analyzed using analytical tools, thereby presenting insights to the readers to make an informed decision from the data.

All of this comes together as social brands and reviews emerge as the most prominent way through which to build trust and loyalty with an audience. Comply with information requirements and privacy laws in regard to legal and ethical considerations. Increase your affiliate marketing efforts by either collaborating with other affiliates or seeking other sources of income outside affiliate marketing.

This book also explained some common mistakes in affiliate marketing and how to avoid them.

This book "Affiliate Marketing Framework" summarized all you need to know, avoid and do as you are growing a successful affiliate marketing business.

Introduction to Affiliate Marketing

Affiliate marketing is an associate business model whereby a relationship exists between a business and others or people that help to promote the products or services of the business. The concept identifies with a pay-for-performance business model; commissions are provided to the affiliates based on results returned, such as sales, leads, or clicks.

Models of Affiliate Marketing

There exist several models of affiliate marketing; each of these has different ways of compensating affiliates:

- Pay-Per-Click (PPC): For every click that their referral links generate, affiliates get paid regardless of whether a consumer purchase was completed or not.

- Pay-Per-Sale (PPS): On each successful purchase made by their referred customer, affiliates get a percentage of the sale price accrued as a commission.

- Pay-Per-Lead (PPL): Here, reward of the commission is on leading basis, usually sign-ups, inquiries, downloads, and other actions excluding direct sales.

Recently, technological advancement has upgraded affiliate marketing tracking and reporting, and the systems used this to manage different programs through the interface usually used to connect merchants to their affiliates.

- Pay-Per-Action (PPA): This is a broader model that includes buying, signing up, or any other specific action that the merchant wants to have done on his website.

Advantages to Affiliate Marketing

- Low Cost to the Merchant: Since merchants are only paying for a result, this is a low-risk way to market.

- Passive Income Creation for Affiliates: Affiliate marketing works on a passive model, thus providing lifetime commission flat on the promotion of something one believes in.

- Scalability: Both merchants and affiliates are able to scale up their operations and venture into new markets.

Affiliate Marketing Ecosystem

At the very center of affiliate marketing is this dynamic ecosystem in which players interact to drive and manage marketing efforts. To move around this complex system, it will help if there is a clearness on the roles, relationships, and processes involved.

Affiliate Marketing Ecosystem Key Players

Merchant (Advertiser): The merchant is more commonly referred to as the advertiser or seller, which is the party that owns what will be promoted. Merchants are afforded the ability to be big companies, small businesses, or even individual entrepreneurs. They create affiliate programs, provide ready material for advertisements, and pay commissions.

Affiliate: It is the person or entity looking to promote the product or service of a merchant, in return for payment in sales, leads and/or clicks generated. They can be bloggers, influencers, content creators, or digital marketers who all look towards leveraging their following or traffic with the aim of driving some to entities while earning in commission.

Consumer/End User: This is the very endpoint of an affiliate's marketing efforts; they interact with the promotional content and hopefully make a purchase or any other desired action that benefits both the merchant and themselves, the affiliate.

Affiliate Network: The affiliate network is an intermediary that helps in the interaction between merchants and affiliates. These affiliate networks provide a tracking function for the affiliate relationships, track the performance of affiliates, and process payments.

It goes on to offer even more tools and resources for its customers to optimize their affiliate marketing campaigns with the help of dependable tracking and reporting.

Tracking and Analytics Platforms: Tools that enable the tracking of affiliate performance, conversions, and aggregating data on marketing efforts; enables learning by merchants and affiliates how to improve on what works.

How the Ecosystem Works

The affiliate marketing ecosystem works through a well-structured process comprising of the following stages:

1. Setting Up the Affiliate Program: The merchant will set up his affiliate program, specifying its terms and conditions, defining commission structures,

and supplying the marketing materials—banners, links, product information, etc.

2. Joining the Program by the Affiliates: Affiliates joining his program or even his network of affiliates get access to unique tracking links and resources to do their promotion. A record of the affiliates is entered into an affiliate program or network and provided with the special links or codes to track in their promotions.

3. Promotion and Traffic Generation: Affiliates promote the products or services of the merchant through different platforms like websites, blogs, social media, or email campaigns.

4. Tracking and Attribution: A consumer first interacts with an affiliate's promotional content, followed by clicking on the tracking link, which may be noted through cookies or tracking mechanisms for attribution to that affiliate.

In simple words, after clicking the link, the affiliate is tracked as having made the activity by the use of a cookie on that consumer's device. All further activities—any activity made—is accounted for under the affiliate.

5. Conversion and Reporting: The completion of the action desired, such as purchasing a product, is tracked and credited to the affiliate's performance through their rightfully deserved commission. The merchant and the affiliate receive detailed reports of the performance and results of the campaigns taking place. In simple terms, the affiliate is said to have converted if the buyer buys the product, the service, or the subscription of your product.

6. Processing Payment: Commissions will, of course, be paid to affiliates in terms of whatever agreement has been made for payment timing. More often than not, the methods of payment are through an affiliate network or with the merchant directly.

Typically, the merchant will process payment and pay the affiliate network, which subsequently pays the affiliate based on pre-defined, agreed terms and amounts.

Key Considerations for Success

Choosing the Right Affiliate Program: The affiliate should engage in programs related to the interests of his audience and that will have good commissions. To a merchant, such programs should be structured in a manner that it encourages good performance while enticing quality affiliates.

- Data and Analytics: Both the merchants and their affiliates are supposed to keep up with tracking and analytics utilities for the sake of noting performance, which will be important in optimizing strategies and driving decisions that are data-driven.

- Compliance and Ethics: Ensuring adherence to the law and upholding the highest ethical standards are critical for building trust and avoiding pitfalls related to disclosure, privacy, and fraud.

Each of the players, understanding the affiliate marketing ecosystem properly, will rabidly foster proper collaboration, offer an optimization of efforts, and lead to mutual win situations. However, you look at it, either you are a merchant trying to enhance the reach or an affiliate looking to maximize earnings, you will avail higher success in affiliate marketing with a good understanding of the ecosystem.

Unearthing the Right Affiliate Programs

Selecting the right affiliate programs is that fine line that separates your revenue potential and your commitment to your promotion goals. Truly, one correct program can keep you on track for super success due to the value offers through its products, commission rates, and proper support. Here is how to go about getting the right affiliate program for your needs:

1. Set Your Goals and Criteria

Do not hurry to start with affiliate programs without understanding what you want to achieve and what you are looking for:

Know your revenue goals: What are your financial objectives? Are you after high commission per sale, or perhaps recurring programs?

Niche alignment: Be sure that the affiliate programs you choose stay true to the niche and audience that concerns you. The products or services must relate to the interests and needs of your target audience.

- Program Type: Choose from the type of affiliate programs that will best work for your strategy: physical products, digital products, services, or a combination.

2. Research Affiliate Networks

The role of the affiliate network is to act between merchants and affiliates, providing the platform for which to cultivate these affiliate relationships. Some popular affiliate networks you can easily join are listed below:

- Amazon Associates: It hosts a large line of products, from gifts to electronics.

It would be great for someone just starting out because of its vast inventory and brand recognition.

- ShareASale: It houses multiple merchants and products and contains tools for tracking and easy-to-use reporting.

- CJ Affiliate (Commission Junction): It has a massive network with big reputed brands, and its reporting features are of the upper grade.

- Rakuten Marketing: A wide range of products and services; the quality of publisher partnerships over quantity, with a focus on performance analytics.

- ClickBank: For selling digital products only. The commission rates at this site are exorbitantly high, which makes it ideal for niches based around information products and e-books.

3. Scrutinize Affiliate Programs

Evaluate the following points separately while scrutinizing affiliate programs:

Commission Structure: Look into the rates of commissions and their terms of payment. The programs may be offering a percentage of the sale, a fixed amount per sale, or even only for leads or clicks.

Product Quality: Inspect whether products or services to be marketed are relevant and of good quality to your audience. Offering quality and relevant products enhances trust and multiply conversion rates.

Cookie Duration: This is otherwise called the tracking window—that's the amount of time after a click that still can get you a commission.

Ensure to always go after longer cookie periods as that will bring you more chances of getting a commission even after the prospective customer had forgotten clicking on your affiliate link.

Support And Resources: Look into the support and resources that you could get from the affiliate program. Truly great programs have in place ready-made marketing materials and training, through which solid support is gained and therefore, an affiliate succeeds.

- Payment Terms: You need to carefully read and understand the payment schedule as well as the minimum payout threshold. Make sure that the terms are reasonable and meet the degree of your financial needs.

- Reputation and Reviews: Search for reviews on the program from other affiliates. See what other affiliates say about a program's reliability or about support quality, among other issues.

4. Apply and Get Started

If you have already identified the targeted affiliate programs, then proceed with the following steps:

Step 1: Signup Join the affiliate programs that interest you. Some of these will need approval, so make sure you are prepared to tell them about your website or strategy in general.

Step 2: Get your affiliate links: Upon approval, you will have an affiliate link or code that you will place unto your promotional content. These track clicks and conversions so that you get credit for your referrals.

- Get the resources: Avail all kinds of resources, from banners to product images and promotional material, that any affiliate program will be able to give.

5. Keep a Track Record and Optimize

Once you have enrolled for affiliate programs, started promoting, keep a record at regular intervals of your performance and also optimize your strategy accordingly:

* Track Performance: Track your clicks, conversions, and commissions with the help of tracking tools and analytics, and identify what kind of products or programs are working for you.

- Optimize Campaigns: Use performance data to optimize marketing efforts. Concentrate on promotions of high-converting products, and keep improving the content and strategies to achieve better results.

- Adjust Partnerships: Be ready to make changes to your affiliate partnerships according to performance outcomes.

If a program doesn't achieve the goals allocated to it, maybe find other alternatives or change your promotional methods.

6. Build Relationships

Building strong relationships with affiliate managers and merchants can pay off as well:

Communication: Stay in close communication with affiliate managers so that you are current with all new offers, promotions, and if changes are added to the affiliate program.

Feedback: Share your experience and in a more subtle way recommend what can be improved on the site. This can earn you special incentives, better support, and other advantages.

Networking: Be active across affiliates and industry contacts for insights and occurrences of new opportunities.

Choosing Your Affiliate Marketing Niche

Selection of the appropriate niche is the most prominent part associated with building a successful affiliate marketing business. It will determine your content, target audience, and the kind of affiliate products or services that you are going to sell. Here is an all-inclusive guide to help you in choosing a niche that best fits your interests, expertise, and market demand.

1. Niche Concept Discernment

A niche is a small specialized segment that caters to some particular type of product or service in the market. In affiliate marketing, choosing a niche simply means it is the area you are going to focus on in which you would be able to provide value and drive in a target audience.

Having clearly defined your niche allows one to differentiate oneself from others and talk more efficiently with your target market.

2. Identifying Your Interests and Expertise

• Personal Interest: Be in a niche in which you are very interested. Your interest will shine through in your content; at the same time, it will keep you motivated over the longer term.

• Expertise: Bring into play any past knowledge or skills. In case you happen to have an expertise in any area, then already there, you can share valuable insights and start building credibility more easily.

- Hobbies and Interests: Consider areas that concern things you do in your free time or things in which you are interested. Your life experience could be everything you need to produce authentic and useful content.

3. Do Market Research

- Market Demand: Do some research on your chosen niche using tools like Google Trends, SEMrush, or Ahrefs. See if there are a good volume of people searching for specific keywords with low-moderate competition.

- Audience Needs: Research what problems or needs your target audience has. Join forums, social media groups, and surveys to know what solutions they are looking for or what kind of information they need.

- Competitor Analysis: Know who your current competitors are in that niche. Check their content, strategies, affiliate products, etc. This can let you recognize any gaps or areas for differentiation.

4. Evaluating Profitability

- Affiliate Programs: Research on the affiliate networks that is currently available and operating in your niche. Know if there are any respectable programs offering good commissions and quality products.

- Monetization Potential: Note how you might monetize your niche. Check through the different revenue models like pay-per-click, pay-per-sale, or pay-per-lead, and see if any of these cases applies best in your case.

- Product Demand: Check for demand in products or services in your niche. High-interest products with recurring interests or needs could possibly help one earn better.

5. Analyzing Competition

- Competitive Landscape: Acquaint yourself with the level of competition in your chosen niche. A highly competitive niche may need much more effort and resources to make a difference, while less competitive niches might allow easier entry but could have lower traffic.

Unique Selling Proposition: Determine one-of-a-kind angle or approach; that's what is going to set your content or promotion above what has already been published. Your Unique Selling Proposition will play a great role in capturing and maintaining your target audience.

6. Testing and Validation

- Pilot Content: Design and share a few pieces of relevant content. Observe audience participation and the kind of feedback you receive.

Affiliate Performance: Join a few affiliate programs and sell their products. Use this as an index that your niche is profitable and that the products are good for your target group.

Adjust and Refine: Refine the niche focus in view of the results obtained from testing. You may need to adjust the content strategy or the target audience or even the affiliate products to better align it with market demand.

7. Long-Term Considerations

• Scalability: Go for a niche with some growth potential. The trends of a niche expanding or evolution in consumer needs will give you more ways to scale your affiliate marketing efforts.

• Sustainability: Make sure the niche is viable for the long term. Stay away from ultra-trendy niches, where — more likely than not — the buzz will fade out in X months. Only go into areas that have ongoing relevance and demand.

- Adaptability: It may be important to adjust your niche if need be. The markets keep changing, and new opportunities sometimes approach; hence, one has to be very flexible to move with shifts that help in maintaining success.

Build Your Online Reputation

Affiliate marketing success depends greatly on having an internet presence. Transforming yourself from an everyday nobody into a digital sensation inspires thousands to follow your footsteps every time they log onto the internet. Comprehensive Guide on How to Build and Keep an Effective Online Presence

1. Define Your Brand

A): Brand identity: Create a brand using the right symbols of art deco that most appeal to your potential customers. This may include your brand name, logo and color scheme from the style guide

Value Proposition: Clearly map out what separates your brand or expression from the rest and why someone should follow/upvote/share etc.

Voice and tone: Your voice is your branding, and somewhere on a spectrum of person or impression you would like to form that finds appeal with your target audience; conversation (having friendly chat), professional mannered but casual suggestion we are established types interested in industry dialog Sharing the stage. Casualness/informal blog posts without pompous setter)

2. Create a Professional Website

Domain Name — Get a domain name that is catchy but also includes your brand as well as the niche you are going into. What is a custom domain such an important thing?

— Web Design: ensure that is how professional as well since interactive to prevent becoming annoyances for their visitor. Most importantly, make sure your website is easy to use and aesthetically pleasing.

Mobile Optimization: Ensure your website is mobile-friendly and swift on all devices This is one place where huge volumes of traffic are from mobile so you cannot miss it.

— Content Management System (CMS): select a CMS as like WordPress to manage & publish the content way better.

3. Develop High-Quality Content

Create a Content Strategy: Which fits your niche and audience interests by now. Regular updates with meaningful data will allow you to strategize and serve promotional pieces as need be.

Content Types — Change up the formats using Blog Posts, Reddit Articles, Videos, Infographics and Podcasts catering to different sections of your audience.

- SEO optimized; makes your content usable for search engines That will increase chances of getting them to higher spots in the SERPs — if, and only If that you can bring organic traffic there.

No value and relevance: Value, because you are here to build that timely bit-sized piece of information or insight for your audience...right? You will need to always provide your audience with a way to learn from, be entertained or at least make something easier for them.

4. Engage with Your Audience

Grow your social media: Keep the rightest profile on a regular platform that fits into slot of target market, such as Facebook, Instagram, Twitter. LinkedIn, Pinterest etc. and regularly post it's branding as well engage its audience.

All of these activities are achieved through the following three community building pillars which encourage comments, forums or social groups so that you can get to talking and start strengthen your tribe. Respond to questions, comments and messages as quickly as possible

Email Marketing Launch an email list to be in contact with your ideal target customer.

Many times, it is easy to get lazy with sending emails out and this is a great way to keep interest up; provide them something of value as always with content, even just an updated or exclusive deal.

5. Utilize SEO Best Practices

Ask the right questions to bring new traffic Use your findings from website analytics,

focus groups and customer surveys to help pull in higher levels of site visits with content that serves prospects according to where they are on their buying journey. If you don't understand what a keyword is (the practice of performing search) I recommend starting here.

– On-Page SEO: Correct your titles, headers, meta descriptions and URL structure address on the pages of a site in an organized and readable fashion.

Ensuring a seamless experience — Technical SEO — Site speed, mobile-friendliness secure connection (HTTPS), Enhanced search engine visibility through improved crawlability and indexability.

– Link Building: Have the technicality on getting high quality links from reputable websites. Doing so cab enhance your site's trustworthiness and in turn, its visibility on search engine.

6. Use data to make better decisions

You can easily track traffic, user behavior and conversion rate through analytical tools like Google analytics. Go through the data in your system and see where things are going right vs. places you need to improve on. Turn insights into a better content strategy, more effective marketing and improved user experience.

7. Think Through Whether to Align or Syndicate

Partner With Influencers: Team up with an influencer or another creator in your niche to get more visibility and credibility. It takes lot of savvy (collaborative content or cross-promotion) to start bringing it in new audiences.

— Affiliates Networking: affiliate marketing forum and network participation. This will help you realize new things and directions to take in your growth as an affiliate.

— Register for Industry events: Sign up to industry conferences, webinars and workshops taking place in your chosen area of study so you can discover recent trends and also meet with gurus in that niche.

8. Ensure Compliance and Trust

– Disclosure and Transparency: Let your readers know. It builds this trust through being transparent, which as you might expect also fulfills the necessary legal norms of proper practice.

You need to make your privacy policy as everything is registered on the server, you should let all of people know what data will be collected and how it will be used?

Secure: Also, don't forget to make your website secure i.e. using SSL and everything that's needed to keep user data safe on the server. Then they trust you more, so make the right impression!!

Driving Traffic to Your Site

If you want them clicking on your affiliate links, first things first: people need to be coming to your site. It means that the more people you get to visit your blog, the more opportunity there is for someone how might resonate with it and buy one of its affiliated products. Kiara Small and I providing an in-depth guide on how you can rewrite from environment to drive traffic visitors back to your site.

1. SEO (Search Engine Optimization)

Keyword Research- Look for low to medium competition keywords that have high search volume and are similar in nature. Time: 5–10 minutes, Tools used: Google Keyword Planner | Ahrefs| SEMrush

On-page: Make sure you incorporate target keywords into content, meta description, headers and URLs as well.

Regular updates and new content will help your site perform better within search engines.

Technical SEO: Faster site, mobile-friendly and secure with https set up your website in a manner that allows search engines to crawl and index the content

2. Social Media Marketing

Choosing the Right Platform: Choose social media platforms that are for your specific niche and where most of who people in demographic go. Use eye-catching visuals, attractive titles and appropriate hashtags for Search boost.

Engage – Comment, discuss and be a part of groups/communities that are related to those you want your brand to appeal.

· Paid Social Advertising: Consider implementing a paid social strategy to reach more people. Facebook and Instagram, for example, allow you to run precisely targeted ad campaigns that could send users headed over your way.

3. Email Marketing

An email list — giving away free resources like eBooks, newsletters and other exclusive offers in exchange for visitors opting into your email.

Dealership Based Dealers Email Marketing Made Easy – triggered campaigns: set up email campaigns that react to individual subscriber interests and actions. Divide your list up so you can send content and promotions to a particular segment of the right people at the right time.

Automated Emails — Use an email service like Mailchimp to schedule automated emails such as welcome series or cart abandonment—this will help you build a relationship with leads over time.

-Stay updated: To make your audience want to check more from you, tell them about added information/promotions/live updates.

4. Content Marketing

Blog — I know alcohol and diet do not go together, but in this case, I mean having a blog with useful informational posts that focus on your area of interest. Use it to siphon off traffic from organic SEO and give your audience some awesome intel.

Guest Blogging: If you are that good then write guest posts for some other decently popular blogs or websites. Outbound link directly to your site, This can bring more traffic and build backlink.

Content Upgrades: Share content that is compatible with visitor emails. This is one of the effective ways to drive traffic and strengthen your email list.

Repackaging of the content: Your old contents should be used in another format for example infographics, video etc. and bring new users to it or regroup traffic.

5. Paid Advertising

Search Engine Ads: Target the keywords on Google or Bing that relate to your offering and brings visitors who are actively looking for a product. Target the relevant Keywords for your niche and Extend Ads

Display Ads — Become a member of display ad network and place banner ads on appropriate website.

However, again — this format of retargeting should add to the other forms as you mentioned in the guise making them convert people that interacted but did not. Retargeting will be handy in gaining back those visitors for better conversions.

6. Influencer Marketing

Get Influencers: have the influencers who has huge followers in your industry.

If they work together, it can draw many visitors to your site and give you credit

Commissioned Reviews/ Articles / Promos: Work with influencers on sponsored content. Use their traffic to get your twitch stream noticed. They will post your products for you and in exchange bring traffic with possible commission on sales.

7. Online Communities and Forums

— Forum Posting: Join forums and online communities about your niche, be active. Provide insights on the forum within your niche and always ensure to put a link back to your site as well when deemed appropriate.

Create your own community: You may want to create an online forum or a Q&A based website like the one you are doing here but concentrated on what is interesting in our niche.

Joint Ventures — Partner with other businesses or affiliates on joint venture opportunities such as sponsoring, co-branding content campaigns etc.

Cross-Promotions: Collaborate with similar websites or related brands to publish content jointly.

Affiliate Programs: Start your own affiliate program for the site in industry — Sign Up to an Affiliate Program When you work with affiliates, you do so to get them involved in selling your products and promoting their audience members a step away from buying on your site.

8. Analyze and optimize

Who do you think is sending the most traffic to this post? Identify the sources...which may be many.... that serve you, and make those outlets your highest yield.

Performance Measurement: Determine the strength of your traffic sourcing strategies. Always monitor the traffic, engagement and conversions stats. Regularly review your strategy and make changes according to the performance data.

Affiliate Email Marketing

Email marketing is a strong ally of affiliate marketers, as it gives you the chance to nurture relationships with your audience and drive traffic to get better conversion rates. By strategically using your email list, you can get the benefit of any affiliate product by preparing a perfect strategy for it. A detailed email marketing guide for affiliates is right here.

1. Growing Your Email List

Even lead magnets in the form of creative free stuff like so-convenient lists or calendars. Free e-books, checklists, articles (yes but hidden behind a paywall), webinars on demand or discount codes are good examples.

-Opt-In Forms Placement: Drive opt-in forms on the homepage This is to help you get more subscribers Make use of either pop-up, inline & even a landing page.

Share your email list on social media Promote specific lead magnets or content upgrades to attract new subscribers.

2. Segmenting Your Email List

– Demographic Information: Divide the list based on demographic data such as age, geo-location or special interests. This way you can customize your content and promotions across all groups.

– Behavioral: Utilize past-purchase data, or whether a subscriber has opened any other email before making targeted segments.

Custom Fields: use custom fields to get any specific information directly from the subscribers. That can uplift the segmenting and customization efforts of your email campaigns.

3. Optimum email campaigns.

Take time to craft subject lines that draw attention in a crowded inbox Avoid sounding like spam and provide clear information about your email contents.

Segmentation: Your Emails need to be broken down, personified! Instead address them by their name and present content related to what they want. Increased Engagement: Email campaigns tend to experience higher engagement levels with personalized emails.

Content & Design: Create well designed, visually inviting emails. Clear Image Layout: Minimal distraction, related images and simple formatting. ideal solution

You may be a marketer, but the one big question you owe it to answer is Why it's important? Product Recommendation Or Special Offer Valuable Insights You Need Something Of Value To Your Audience.

– Call to actions (CTAs)- Your email should have great CTAs, make them big Push subscribers to click on affiliate links, visit your site», buy.

4. Power Of Email Automation

Leverage on building a welcome series for your new subscribers. This might look like a sequence of emails introducing your brand, providing free value and delivering offers.

Drip Campaign Leveraging: It enables you to nurture each lead and thus perfect the probable results of every single one over a course of time. Use a series of informational autoresponder emails — to lead them through the journey and ultimately, they will buy from you.

Recover sales which could have been lost because of visitors who may not purchase by using abandoned cart emails for eCommerce affiliates. Initiate cart abandonment series and push those sales with an incentive to convert.

Re-engagement campaigns: If possible, entice them to take another look at your content/offers and use an exclusive discount if necessary.

5. Promoting Affiliate Products

Product Reviews and Recommendations- Share detailed reviews or recommendations about affiliate products. Convey benefits, features, and USPs.

- Course creation: Create a course integrating affiliate products Such as how-to guides, tutorials or case studies which might provide proof in terms of the prevalent benefit from products.

Seasonal Campaigns: Unless your business is all-season, calibrating promotions according to the seasonal events (holidays and special occasion) You just need to customize your offers and content according time of the year.

6. Testing and Optimizing

— A/B Testing: Test your subject line, content or a CTA on different emails. Use the results to have an improved campaign that works wonderfully.

Analytical And Tracking: Monitor email marketing analytics, click-through rate conversion rates/lists.

Data Driven Changes: Make data driven changes to your email marketing campaigns, so you can keep evolving according to how they perform. Increase Performance By Laser-Targeting, Content and Design.

7. Maintaining Compliance and Best Practices

Compliance: Make sure your email marketing is acting in accordance with regulations such as GDPR, CAN-SPAM, or CCPA. Embed an unsubscribe mechanism in all mailings, and honor them within 10 days.

Use Double Opt-In With Email Subscribers — this helps reduce your risk of having spam traps. Make sure your emails offer something of value, without bombarding subscribers with too many messages.

8. Forged and Manage Relationships

- Communicate: Keep in touch with your subscribers and balance staying top of mind with not becoming an intrusion in their inbox.

— Feedback and Engagement — Get your subscribers to engage with/utilize feedback. Collect findings and optimize your email content /strategy for free via direct response/surveys.

Community Building: Encourage a community sense through responsiveness and engagement with subscribers leading to loyalty. Make it easier for them to talk with you and among themselves.

Turning your visitors into sales

Optimizing for conversions will be key a crucial part of overall success. And depending on strategy, how to generate leads and close deals is about integrated content with focus-driven design followed by a spotless experience. Here is hand-written overall details, to jump-start your optimization process In order to increase the conversion rates.

1. Optimize Your Landing Pages

The Single Value Proposition: Your value proposition should clearly communicate what the offer is and how it helps the visitor. It sometimes just flat-out means reinforcing why, what and how you are better than the other guys.

The Bad. — Attention Grabbing Headlines: You need a headline that will draw attention and speaks to the pain points of your visitors Double check these are relevant to your referrals.

Visuals: Visual can be a deciding attention trigger, it makes an example for the visitors by showing them upfront what product or services are being offered this could mean good quality images (or videos) of your actual products. Images: Images should be distinctive and pertinent to demonstrate the value of what you offer.

Strong CTA: Inserting a call-to-action leading visitors exactly to the action that you want them to take (purchase, free trail etc.) • Use active verbs and let your intention well known.

2. Enhance User Experience (UX)

– Fast Loading Time: Your website and landing pages should load extremely fast. Slow load times can lead to a huge turnover of bounced traffic and losing revenue.

User-Focused Data Entry Forms: If conversion is by form completion (e.g., lead gen or sign up), ensure the forms are intuitive. Do Not Ask For Too Much Info.

3. Applying Social Proof and Trust Signals

Commercial Customer Reviews — Introduce the good portions of customer reviews and feedback to your page. This does for you in building Social Proof, and convinces them that they can trust to buy from your site.

Clinical trials & results: Share with the audience about your RCTs, cohort studies or systematic reviews and meta-analysis. Highlight Applied Solutions and Evidenced Outcomes

Trust Badges and Certifications: You will need to incorporate trust badges, simply because the location wants your information protected and associated with an understanding that no one apart from business would have access of a transaction.

Media Quotes/Awards: List any media citations, awards or other accolades that add credibility to your product/brand.

4. Personalization and targeting

Dynamic Content: Display different content based off of user behavior, location or referral source i.e. showing custom promotions on past engagement/visit

Retargeting Campaigns-Improve your conversions by reengaging visitors that have been on your site without making a purchase Display Ads — Relevant ad for retargeted ads reminders of the offer.

— Behavioral Triggers: This permits you to ship trigger-primarily based emails, which include abandoned carts or surfing history.

5. Create Irresistible Offers

Special Promotions and Discounts — Give a deal that can only be activated during the provided time period or special promotion Focus on what they stand to gain from inaction instead.

Free Trials or Samples: Give them a taste of the pudding without actually eating it through free trials and samples. You might be able to mitigate the damage of this apparent risk in your investment.

— Elastic Baskets: Netflix-like subscription model (daily, weekly or yearly) that provide over value in less cash. Show how the other products or features expand on that initial offer.

6. Leverage high-converting sales funnels

Create a Lead Nurturing Model —Deliver additional content to lead them through the sales funnel Create value, handle objections and build over time.

Conversion Pathways —Craft concise pathways that move the visitor along from awareness stage to decision-making; Every flow within the funnel is visitor-focused.

Follow Up Sequences – Utilize follow-up email sequences or retargeting ads to keep showing your offer in front of those who have not purchased yet. Offer more information or an incentive for visitors to convert.

7. Implement A/B Testing

– A/B Testing: Use different split tests on the landing pages, CTAs, headlines and offer. Experiment with different ins, check which works for you.

Break down Results: Data From A/B Tests guides Design & Content decisions Test, test and always examine what gets you the highest conversions!

8. Create and Save Connection

Keep talking to your audience: Keep commenting, posting on social media and email prospects. Nurture leads: Building stronger relationships can also grow trust with prospects and transition them down the sales pipeline to conversions.

Provide Value: Share valuable information, tools with visitors to help them make educated decisions Fast, professional resolution of issues and questions

Customer Feedback: Conduct detailed research about what customers currently need as well as anticipate their future needs so that you can accurately monitor the feedback received. By having this data, you can fine-tune your offers and increase conversions.

9. Track and Measure Performance

– Metrics – Monitor critical KPIs (conversions, CTA rates, bounce rate) these are all essential measures of pushes in the proper direction. – UX Design; The Off-Ramp Introduction100 metrics went over using tools like Google Analytics.

Trend Analysis: Use performance data to see if you are implementing the best practices or introducing better tools. Find out what's performing in conversions and where can you make improvements.

– Adaptive Strategies: Build according to performance data and keep evolving. Point out corrections in where necessary and reinforce the process that are giving you feedback.

Affiliate Marketing Tracking + Analytics

To measure the success of your affiliate marketing efforts and optimize performance, as well for making data-driven decisions you need effective tracking and analytics. Knowing what works will help you iterate on your strategies to improve ROI and drive towards marketing goals. This is the ultimate affiliate marketing tracking and analytics guide.

1. Setting Up Tracking

Affiliate Tracking Software- You can use affiliate tracking software or you can provide an offer through the secure purchase network that is included in many all-in-one platform like Click Funnels.

UTM Parameters: Append UTM parameters to your affiliate URLs so you can track how each campaign performs in Google Analytics.

Use UTM parameters to identify which source, medium and campaign brought the traffic.

Link Shorteners: Link shortening tools can be valuable because they oftentimes offer built-in tracking (i.e. Bitly, Pretty Links) to track things like click-through rates and other Click Meter metrics.

2. Key Metrics to Track

– Clicks: The number of clicks on your affiliate links is helpful for knowing trends and traffic generation.

Conversions: Track conversions or completed actions influenced by affiliate referrals (purchases, sign-ups).

Conversion Rate: Determine the conversion rate by dividing the number of completions with clicks This is a measure of how well your visitors are converting into sales.

Revenue: Overall revenue from the same affiliate sales It will help you to know the profitability of your affiliate marketing efforts.

– AOV (Average Order Value): Commonly this average order value is shown by dividing revenue to number of orders placed. So, this metric will help know how shopping is done in your viewers.

Cost Per Acquisition (CPA): Find out the cost per acquisition by dividing total marketing costs to convert So that you could measure whether, quality and bring brand name promotions efficiently.

Return on Investment (ROI) – Calculate ROI by evaluating the revenue earned from affiliate sales to the expense of your marketing efforts. This can help you evaluate the effectiveness of your affiliate marketing efforts overall.

3. Telemetry tracking tools and platforms

Google Analytics: Track and monitoring the entire system of operations inside Google management area. Create goals and funnels for tracking conversions and user behavior.

Affiliate Networks: Make it a practice to leverage the tracking and reporting tools made available by affiliate networks. These assists may include clicks, conversions or driven commissions and more.

Marketing Automation Platforms: Landing pages are often integrated with a marketing automation platform such as HubSpot or Marketo, which allows for more advanced tracking and analytics on email campaigns, lead nurturing and customer behavior.

Heatmaps and Session Recordings: Hotjar or Crazy Egg offer heatmapping solution with session recordings to see the most important visitors clicks on your site.

4. Analyzing Data

— Read Performance Reports (from your affiliate tracking) or network at regular intervals. Use metrics like clicks, conversions and revenue to measure comprehensive performance.

Campaign Performance: Monitor the performance of each campaign and compare clicks, conversions rates and ROI across different sites. Determine which campaigns are working best

Traffic Sources: Examine where your traffic is coming from (search engines, social media and email ...), to see what sources make up more of that audience, and which channels are the most performant ones.

Analytics Audience Behavior: Use data measurement tools to understand the behavior of visitors on your site.

Conversion Funnels: Test you conversion funnels to find where your visitors are dropping off and reasons for abandoning the process. This increases user journey efficiency and your conversions.

5. Making Data-Driven Decisions

Optimize Campaigns: Apply learnings from your analysis into campaign tweaks. Fine-tune targeting, messaging or offers that seem to strike a chord with your audience.

— Test and Iterate: A/B test, experiments with different approaches Data + Informed Decisions → iterate on the strategies

Invest your budget: Allocate my marketing budgets according to how well each channel and campaign is doing.

6. Reporting and Communication

Regular Reports — Make regular reports to monitor the progress and keep stakeholders

informed on the latest insights. Key Metrics; Performance Summaries & Actionable Recommendations.

Dashboard Tools — With this tool, you can create visual representations of your data by using dashboard tools like Google Data Studio or Tableau. Be it the analytics dashboards which give you a view of core metrics and trends.

Feedback Loop: Form a feedback loop with team members or partners. Use these reports to provide insights, review performance and work together on strategies for improvement.

7. Privacy and Compliance

Data Privacy: Make sure you're tracking and analyzing correctly — check for data privacy regulations such as GDPR, CCPA or other similar laws Get your approvals and respect the data.

Cookie Policies - Have a cookie policy and inform users that cookies are being used, while tracking. Give users proper choices to manage their cookies.

Social proof & reviews in affiliate marketing

In the world of affiliate marketing, nothing creates sales [and can take your roof off] like social proof and reviews. By highlighting endorsements and displaying testimonials, you can give more legitimacy to your business in the eyes of potential leads which will help boost conversions whilst at same time promoting positive user experiences. Keep reading to find out how you can make great use of social proof and reviews and give your affiliate marketing a heads up.

1. Understanding Social Proof

Peer Influence: nurtured via the principles of social proof- i.e. people will copy what others do to help decide how they themselves should act In marketing that means we use testimonial, reviews and endorsements to build credibility which results in trust.

- Types of Social Proof:

Testimonials & Reviews – testing + real feedback from people who actually used it.

Your personal testimonies or testimony of other customers/influencers like positive remarks about the product, service.

Case Studies — Provide in-depth use cases exhibiting the solution solving specific problems or innovations.

Referred by Social Media: Comments, shares or endorsements from social media signers

– Trust Badges and Certifications: Visual indicators of trust such as security certifications or industry awards.

2. Gather and showcase Reviews.

– Request Reviews: whether you follow-up with an email, ask on social media or provide some kind of benefit return in exchange for reviews help your audience review! Keep the process brief and user-friendly.

Keep Your Feature Reviews Prominently Show up reviews on both website and landing page.

Use Review Aggregators: Aggregate and display reviews from Trustpilot, Yelp or Google Reviews. You also can find widgets or plugins to add reviews on your website from these platforms itself.

Feature User Generated Content: Provide incentives to your customers for snapping and sharing (picture or video). Then highlight this content on your website or social media sites to create a record of authentic Social Proof.

3. Compelling Testimonials — How to Write Them

Encouraging Testimonials: Choose testimonials which solved problems or highlighted primary use cases for the product. They communicate better to certain audiences in different formats.

Disclosure: disclose a reviewer name photo thumbnail + occupation — Adding reviewers personal details makes them more convincing A lengthy testimony is far more attractive than blanket statement or something by an anonymous.

Leverage Case Studies Rather than more of a vague concept like imagining how people use your solution or just having an in-depth understanding on their portfolio and industry with real-world applications.

4. How to Employ Social Media Impressions

• Watch Your Brand Mentions: Make sure to monitor tools on brand mentions if you are promoting a specific product or service.

Hand-in/Social Network Activity — Secondly, opt to share a valuable quote can be one of your most effective influencers investment marketing low hanging fruits.

It does this by showing live examples of use cases and assisting in trust build up.

Work With Influencers: Teamed up with influencer marketing plans to partner yourself directly close by the tools that can effectively give casual references and guidelines from their real-life.

5. Trust Badges & Certifications

– Make Use of Security Badges: If there is a security payment system or data protection for the product/service that an affiliate wants to promote, then use highly credible security badges on your website.

Industry Award Section: share all the awards or certifications product/service acquires Industry recognition can go a long way in building credibility and trust.

– Partner Logos | Displays the brand's logo of products or services utilized for a credibility aspect: They logos also act as welcomed endorsements from partners.

6. Creating A Social Proof Strategy

Social Proof Across The Funnel: Incorporate social proof elements across different stages of your funnel — starting from landing pages to checkout pages. To achieve mistrust and friction, the same methodology should be used.

A/B Test Social Proof Elements: social proof can take many different shapes, and where you place it also might drive your total conversion rate. A/B testing lets you optimize it, but ultimately the system does something like 100 tests and then makes choices based off that data.

Extension -> Keep it Fresh: Make sure that your social proof is current with the most recent positive reviews, testimonials, endorsements etc. Social Proof works only if fresh and timely.

Genuine: Show social proofs that reflect real experiences of users, and how it impacts their life. As we often forget in the digital world, caring and pretending to care are HUGE on social media — but so is mistrust; more than 50% of those surveyed said that an organization acting insincere would make them stop following their account.

7. Addressing Negative Reviews

Use the feedback: Convert negative reviews into potential points of improvement. Solve recurring issues and inform how you are changing; make it clear that your company is acting responsibly.

Getting them to respond positively: -- Of course this is one method, so if you meet a customer or client expectation of what they expect from your business and that action is adequate for their cause for grievance then also ask those same clients / customers leave an updated review which included Testimonial As we all know, good habits can only be built upon the roots and more success than ever to do them again.

7. Social Proof

Conversion Rate: Look at your conversion rate before and after throwing in some additional social proof intelligences. Learn How Social Proof Can Impact Sales.

Measuring Engagement Metrics: Take out all common variations from your on-site volume by analyzing post-click metrics (CTR, time spent on site, bounce rate) to understand if social proof is delivering the engagement of visitors with a different impact.

- User feedback on social prodigious elements/ collect user survey.

Ethical and Compliant Affiliate Marketing

Now, the internet is a great facility to make money from homes through affiliate marketing but it needs compliance and ethics by fundamental/copyleft/mandatory principles of fairness or transparency across all industries i.e., legal racket. Breaking these norms not only risks breaking the trust of your audience but also from partners and regulators. The Ultimate Guide to Compliance and Ethics in Affiliate Marketing.

1. Understanding the Compliance Elements

Regulatory Framework: Get to know the affiliate marketing rules located in your jurisdiction. Common regulations include:

Federal Trade Commission — The affiliate relationships disclosure and misleading advertising prohibited in the United States.

California Consumer Privacy Act: In the state of California, CCPA prescribes rules related to consumer privacy and their personal data rights.

Here are some basic rules that you should be aware of: - Affiliate Program Policies: You need to review each affiliate program terms and conditions. Understanding specifically what your affiliate requires in terms of compliance — promotions and disclosures are key to this solution.

2. Affiliate Disclosure

– Full Disclosure: Be sure to always post who you are an affiliate for in a clear and concise manner. Be transparent: When you promote affiliate products, FTC guidelines require that your audience is clearly informed and notified in advance about any potential earning if they purchase the product.

- Where to Include Disclosures: Place disclosures where consumers are likely to notice them, for example at the top of a blog post or near an affiliate link. Make the disclosure simple and conspicuous.

- Disclosure Language: Clearly explain to readers the nature of your affiliate relationship. These include simple language like "As an Amazon Associate, I earn from qualifying purchases" and more fleshed out versions.

3. Circumvent Deceptive Practices

Honest Reviews: Write honest reviews of the products and services; Do not even think about overselling the benefits of your product or service, nothing will have people running away faster than a few skeptics accusing you and what you do are scammers.

– Genuine Suggestions: Always recommend a product or service you have actually used/testing/researched.

Metric Transparencies: If you include performance metrics or data in your promotions, make sure they are accurate and verifiable. This not only hurts credibility but also violates rules and regulations.

4. Data Privacy and Security

Data Collection: Make sure you are collecting and processing personal information in accordance with applicable data protection laws. Ask for explicit consent when collecting information personal data

Data Security: Ensure protection of personal data your visitors and customers. Always have a secure connection (SSL)and update your software periodically, to ensure that you maintain robust data protection habits.

Privacy Policies: Explain to visitors what data your site collects, as well how does it use and where protect this data — In writing these policies show users that they have the option of opting out or requesting removal.

5. Ethical Marketing Practices

Respecting User Experience: We ask that you not be overly aggressive in pushy or disruptive advertising. Make sure your promos add to the experience rather than take away from it.

- Authenticated Reporting: Since affiliates commissions and traffic are accounted for. Inaccurate performance data might not only be legally problematic but it can also harm relationships with affiliate networks.

To Mitigate Conflicts of Interest: Flag potential conflicts that may present a conflict with your impartiality. Tell your audience, for instance, if you have an economic stake in a product or service.

6. Working with Affiliates

Transparency with Affiliates: Be open about your relationship to affiliate program managers and partners.

Talk about what you need or expect, promotional plans for your event and any problems that arise.

Consistency with the Rules: Abide by all trademarks of affiliate programs. Promotions, brand guidelines and advertising compliance.

Disputes: Respond to affiliate programs disputes/issues professionally and swiftly Communicate and document so conflicts are resolved.

7. Legal Considerations

-Contractual Obligations: Be sure to read and comply with the terms of all affiliate agreements you join. Make sure that you know what your obligations and rights are under the contract

- Tax Compliance: Be familiar with which taxes you might need to pay on your affiliate income. Maintain good record-keeping for earnings and consider consulting with a tax professional to help ensure compliance with state and federal taxation.

This includes but is not limited to -International Regulations: If you are international the laws of each country that you target apply so be sure you're in compliance.

8. Learning and Evolution

– Stay Updated: Federal guidelines for affiliate marketing are continuously updated so you need to stay informed about best practices and new regulations. Stay updated with industry news and webinars as well as through professional networks.

Adapt Strategies — Move along with the trend and change your marketing strategies accordingly to follow up new regulations or increasing ethical behavior. Being responsive to changes will be key for maintaining compliance and credibility.

Training and Resources: Educate yourself, as well your team to be knowing all you need for compliance in affiliate marketing with a correct ethic practice.

Affiliate Marketing Business Scalability

Focusing on the right things is what aids to grow your affiliate marketing business generates more traffic, revenue gains and operations processes that are operationally more efficient (but frankly not less cumbersome). The Ultimate Guide to Scaling Up Your Affiliate Marketing Business.

1. Current Strategies for Optimizing the Studying

Performance Indicate — Track your performance of existing affiliate campaigns. These are the only key result areas you need to be analyzing: conversion rate, where they came from and ROI (return on investment).

Scale Top Performing Campaigns: focus on scaling the campaigns that are already working best. From there, try expanding budgets while targeting in on your audience and variations to see if you can improve performance.

Just remove the strategy or amend it, if not getting desired results. Step3- Weed Out Less Effective Strategies: Any that is doing nothing to help your business can be weeded out (amended) and get back in track. Direct Resources based on Higher potential-based Opportunities.

2. Diversify Traffic Sources

Increase your Audience: Or simply try new mediums as social media, influencer marketing or other search engines. Because of this, diversification protects us from putting too many eggs in a single basket.

– Monetize using Paid Advertising: Run paid advertising campaigns with Google Ads, Facebook ads and other platforms related to your industry.

Content Marketing: Check for more type of assets sort then simply blogging- blogs, videos, infographics & podcasts — Post High-Quality(attractive) Content Consistently.

3. Nurture Relationships

Nurturing those relationships with people (organizations/partners) to increase recurring sales.

– Connect with Industry Powerhouses: Develop industry wide power house relationships, lateral synergies as well as Peak Performers. Collaborate on content, campaigns and endorsements for broader reach and credibility.

– Join More Affiliate Programs: You Should Go and join other affiliate programs in your niche like, for instance. By diversifying your selection of affiliate partners, you open up a new avenue to revenue opportunities.

– Improve Your Terms: Leverage your performance data to be able to improve how you are performing with current affiliates.

Negotiate for Higher Commission, Much More Generous Promotions or Top-Notch Support.

4. Automation And Operational Simplification

Automation tools — Introduce automation such as email marketing, social media posting and even reports. Copying and pasting content for marketing efforts ---> time saver maintaining consistency using automation

Enhancing Workflow: Keep the workflow on track by utilizing project and collaboration tools.

Analytics Tools - Utilize the most advanced analytics tools to measure success, identify trends and produce actionable insights.

5. Continue your education

You can spend money on courses, webinars or even live events to expand your knowledge and improve yourself.

– For SEO, Content built etc. as well-paid efforts e.g., hire experts or consultants for one time funding Come on faster and earlier than ever before can help achieve your goals.

Build a Team — as n when business scales, one should create team for different responsibilities like content writing customer support or marketing. As mentioned, experts can manage the recovery of an increased volume while working to grow your volume simultaneously (without bribing you with 24/7 availability demands).

6. Enhance Customer Experience

Personal Interactions: Use data for tailored customer interaction and suggestions.

Be responsible: Provide top notch customer service Answer queries, address issues as quickly as you can to gain the trust so that new clients / followers are comfortable with your platform.

Collect consumer feedback: Create customer response surveys inhouse to determine and tune you what their needs.

7. Scale Content and Outreach

— Additional Content Channels: Posting your content on a variety of places, ranging from guest blog posts and general syndication to social media channel.

Repurposing Content — You can do things you are already doing and transform them into other formats that can be consumed by different types of people. Change the format, turn a blog post into video -an infographic- hell go even further and make that article one of your podcast episodes.

8. Be Aware of Scaling And Optimize Your Channels

Monitoring Scaling Metrics—Be sure to track effective scaling metrics, like more traffic or a higher conversion rate. You should, therefore watch them carefully and adjust your scaling efforts accordingly.

— Course-Correction: Strategies need to be flexible and changed with data-analysis or market conditions so always ready to course-correct. But to scale in this way, of course, flexibility and adaptability are essential.

9. Reach out to New Markets & Audience

— Expand Geographies: If you sell in < 1/5 of the US, look into selling everywhere. Model regional practices and note what could be implemented in light of local taste, tradition and laws.

Find New Demographics — Determine if there are any other demographic segments that should be interested in your product/service. Furthermore, tailor your marketing to their demographics too.

Build Niche Offerings: Develop offerings or sub-brands that cater to particular interests in your target market.

In short, it is the ultimate answer to your e-commerce woes and enables you to pick up a specialization in any complete one of its types where only few others offer that unique something.

10. Compliance and ethics

Compliance: Compliance is not about operating in accordance with the language of different local, state or federal laws and private standards bodies. Maintain your understanding of relevant laws and regulations affecting affiliate marketing campaigns.

Maintain Ethical Standards —Always keep your marketing ethical... Be transparent, truthful and uphold your standards

• Monitor Compliance: Regularly audit your practices and those of the affiliates to avoid non-compliant actions in respect not just lawfulness but also ethical conducts.

Affiliate Marketing with Influencers and Partners

Collaborate with Influencers & partners to sky rocket the effort of your affiliate marketing and it allow you gain credibility, create unbelievable growth. A strategic plan, clear communication and management of each relationship. So, here we have compiled all the best practices that might help you while working with influencers and partners in affiliate marketing —

1. Finding The Best Influencers & Partners

Define Your Goals: You must have a clear idea of what you want to achieve from any influencer collaboration or partner before starting, be it raising brand awareness, kickstarting sales or outreach new markets.

Online Influencer Research: Locate influencers who have similar values, target market and niche as you. Ensure that they have strong engagement, quality content and the correct audience.

— Identify Potential Partners: Based on your offerings, look for similar affiliate partners or businesses. Find other businesses that would be serving your ideal customers, and already have a strong reputation in their industry.

Evaluate Fit- Regardless of which influencers or partners you decide to work with, ensure that the ones you do consider are truly resonating with their user base. The activities of the influencers or partners should resonate with your message and brand values. Successful collaborations will always come from authenticity.

2. Building Strong Relationships

Professional Extension: If you really like what the page gives and see a mutually beneficial partnership, then reach out to influencers who can promote your stuff in an email with some example value add that will benefit them linked in below as well.

— Define Scope of Work: Lay out what you expect, work wise and payload, deliverables timelines etc. compensation as well Make sure, that both sides understand very well what they have to take care of and what can be expected out from this collaboration.

-Communication: Make sure that there is open and honest communication throughout the partnership. Every question, doubt or issue should be settled to build a proper bond of trust and work fluently with each other.

3. Creating Effective Consortium Agreements

— Comprehensive Contracts: Start with strong contracts that specify project terms, pay rates, structure of cooperation and deliverables; performance expectations regarding content guidance on compliance and legal requirements. The terms must be reviewed and agreed upon by both parties.

– Require Distribution Disclosure: This is a term that will display in the contracts. That way, it will count as a legal obligation requirement filled (such as the affiliate marketing and endorsements compliance by FTC guidelines).

4. The Art (And Skill) Of Managing Collaborations

Specifying Performance Metrics: Define them in vivid manner that what are the performance metrics and KPIs signaling towards success of collaboration. These might encompass click through rates, conversions, social media engagement or the ROI.

Detail Creative: communicate exactly what are the content creation process, branding placement and messaging constraints Ensure influencers and partners genuinely are following the standards you set for them, and making sure it stays consistent across everything they do.

Monitoring Performance: Track performance for the influencers and their campaigns with help of analytics tools.

You need to evaluate the performance by tracking traffic, conversions and other engagement metrics.

Support and Feedback: Full-cycle support with feedback on the go. Actively resolve issues or challenges to support partner realization of maximum performance potential.

Reward — such as offering bonuses or incentives — or (as simple as it may sound) more opportunities for top talent influencers and partners to regularly engage.

5. Utilizing influencers content

• Repurpose Content: With permission, repackaged influencer content for use on your owned-marketing channels including websites, social media or email campaigns. Otherwise, it could potentially increase the stride range of influence and effectiveness.

Website / social media: Testimonials, case studies or examples of content created can be given. You could even showcase your collaborations on a site or through social media.

Get Involved with Content: Participate actively with the content of any collabs you do, as well as other partners. Make comments, share and re-post their posts to improve the visibility of account and connect with them.

6. Success Metrics and Tweak Strategies

7.

Measure Results — Reviewing the performance data from your influencer and partner campaigns to see whether they fell (or didn't fall) in line with your goals as set. Assess what is needed.

- Strategy Refinement: Implement insights onto your strategy for future collaborations. Review what really worked and work on the shortcomings to enhance your method.

— Feedback: Get fully honest feedback from the influencer and partner, then do whatever it takes to make them happy. Leverage their insights to streamline processes while deciding their direction for future engagements.

8. Influencer and Partner Collaborations at Scale

Growing the Network — It is a continuous process of search for new influencers and partners to do partnerships with. Reduce exposure to the various new audience and markets by expanding into a network.

- Cultivate Partnerships: Create relationships with influencers and top-performing affiliates. Establish ongoing partnerships top ensure continuity & greatest reach.

Test new collaboration formats (e.g. joint webinars, co-branded products or exclusive events).

9. Reinforced Compliance and Ethical Practices

- Act Legally: All of your joint activities need to be compliant with the many laws and regulations. Make sure that affiliate relationships are properly disclosed and compliant with advertising standards.

- Privacy: When working together, handle any resulting personal data in a manner that is consistent with each individual's laws of Data Protection. Develop sound data protection policies and protocol.

How to monetize beyond affiliate links

Most of the commissions made through affiliate marketing are made only when an organization is being promoted through unique affiliate links. Advanced affiliates will tell you about monetization beyond this. Here's how to promote more than just affiliate links so that you earn even more while you're delivering more value to your audience. The Ultimate Guide to Monetizing Your Platform

1. Sponsored Content & Advertorials

Write posts that are relevant to the niche you are in and serve, bringing good quality value to your readers with the sponsored product or service in mind.

Advertorials: Write advertorials, which are articles that combine a typical ad with an editorial piece. Articles you write to offer value, give them information, and entertain subtly with a promotion of your brand and product.

2. Selling Digital Products

That is, if you can develop e-books on subjects related to your niche, it could be how-to guides, or it could be industry insights, for example.

Online Courses: Profit by selling online courses or webinars! Monetize Your Knowledge to Offer Learning in your Niche

Printables Templates: Selling digital printables like planners, checklists, templates. Those can be very high-margin products that pay you passive income month after month.

3. Subscribers:

Some Free But Most with Premium Memberships

Member Sites – Start a membership site that provides access to high-value content, resources or members-only community. Offer something of immense value within your articles, videos or discussion forums.

Subscription Services: Develop a subscription model for regular delivery of content or updates. Different levels of Membership Offer membership at different levels that offer distinct benefits. In this way, you'll be able to entice various segments of audiences and monetize at a higher return.

4. Physical Product Sales

– Ecommerce Store: You will also own an e-commerce store that will sell physical products in your niche. This can be branded merchandise, niche products, or palettes of handpicked items.

Drop shipping: Collaborating with suppliers for selling out products without inventory ownership Drop shipping is a way to sell many different items without having to stock them up beforehand.

Affiliate Products — While affiliate links always remain, in the rhetoric, you could bundle them together and/or make similar offer available, but only to your audience, through your own online store.

5. Hosting Events and Webinars

Paid Webinars: Host events with some regularity around key topics for your audience and charge admission to attend. Webinars are either live, recorded or a combination of interactive/educational value.

Workshops & Seminars: Hosting / carrying out live workshops or seminars offline/ online helps you network and get valuable experience firsthand.

- Conferences: Creating and running new conferences or other industry-related events. These said cannot be compared with the larger events, where there are multiple speakers running their very sessions that are free for sponsorship and also 'buy a ticket to'.

6. Licensing and Royalties

— Content rights licensing — License content to other publishers, media, or brands License Your Work for a Potential Future of Passive Income.

Royalty Deals: Strike up royalty deals with other organizations for products or content you develop. Whether that is royalties for books, courses, or any other material you design.

7 Advertising and Sponsorship

Direct Sponsorship: Approach brands and ask them to sponsor you directly for advertising or product placement on your site, as well as on social media. You can separately negotiate terms and set your own rates from the sponsors.

Podcast Sponsorships — If you host a Podcast, commercialize it by getting shows sponsored on a per episode or even a segment basis. Monetize Podcast Sponsored Content & Ads.

8 Affiliate Marketing Programs

Build Your Own Affiliate Program: Build your own affiliate program to allow other promoters of your products and services for a payout on commissions. It does help maximize outreach and put excellent use to other marketing strategies.

– Joint Venture With Other Affiliates – Work together with other affiliates on a joint venture. Each affiliate cross-promoted the other affiliate's products and services.

9 Mentoring and Coaching

— Consulting Services – Provide coaching based on whatever it is you master. Give solid recommendations, share strategy consultations, business growth opportunity.

– Coaching Programs: Develop training programs to support those in your niche to also consider a second income.

— Mentorship: Develop mentorship programs to help those who also might one day become your competition ......with skills you have taught them.

10. Crowdfunding and Donations

Crowdfunding Campaigns — Run a campaign on a platform like Kickstarter or Indiegogo to raise money for new projects or business ventures. Backers will be incentivized with rewards or perks for supporting your ideas.

- You will accept donations and run crowdsourcing efforts in a bid to keep your content or work alive. With services like Patreon, fans can pay artists directly for exclusive content or other means of access.

11. Affiliate Marketing Resource and Tools

Building Tools: Create and sell tools or resources that make life easier for other marketers (e.g. SEO software, content planning templates, marketing apps).

Educational Resources: Guides, courses or training offerings to help educate affiliate marketers with how best practices. You then become an expert and you offer a great resource for people in your industry.

12. Licensing Your Content

- License Content: You have an opportunity to license your content to other boards and brands. The content is yours, but on the other hand, it can be used by people whereas you still have an income being generated from it.

Content Syndication: This is where you take pre-existing content, which is yours, of course, and then send it out on other platforms or through varying media channels to help take you further while generating an extra revenue stream through licensing your content.

14 Common Mistakes to Avoid with Affiliate Marketing

The potential for earnings are absolutely ginormous with affiliate marketing, but there several mistakes people make that cause them to get nowhere. The better you can understand and avoid these pitfalls, the greater overall reach/perhaps profitability your efforts will be. So below is an important whitepaper on affiliate marketing mistakes and tips to avoid them.

1. Choosing the Wrong Niche

Mistake #1: Choosing a general category you are not interested in or well-versed can result in low engagement and bad marketing.

How to Avoid:

Research and specialize — Pick a niche; Find an area that interests you, utilize your base knowledge but also what the market demands.

Niche down and have a look which niches that there is more than enough audience interest in as well as affiliate opportunities.

Find profitable niches: Get to know about competition, general commission rates as well demand of products.

2. Low-Quality Product Promotion

Mistake #2: Promoting low-quality or irrelevant product to your audience which will be a mark on builder that reduces the visitor percentage.

How to Avoid:

Try the products or experience them for yourself in order to endorse it Make sure they are quality products that deliver real value to your audience.

Go Through Reviews: Analyze various reviews and user feedback that has been left by previous customers to determine how good the product is.

3. Ignoring SEO and Content Quality

Mistake #3: Ignoring SEO and letting crappy, mundane content rank as low-value will be ranked by search engines to the best (the worst) extent so do your audience.

How to Avoid:

Content Optimization: Make sure you optimize the content for proper keywords using keyword research tools. Based on creating valuable, educational and entertaining content that meet the needs of your audience.

- Keep it fresh: Always keep the content next to relevance. Content Refresh And Review Always refresh and reevaluate your content so that it continues to serve its purpose for SEO.

4. Ignoring the Target Audience Needs and Preferences

Mistake #4: If you are unaware of your audience at all, or otherwise fail to recognize and respect what that audience prefers in this realm — then any promotion is entirely irrelevant.

How to Avoid:

Send Surveys: polls, feedback forms... gathers information to make tailored offers. Once developed, craft content and marketing largely around those accommodations.

— Interaction with Your Audience: Respond to comments and messages on posts, social media platforms about your content or through email in order for you to get feedback from them.

5. Ignoring Everything But Traffic

Mistake #5: Failure to convert (if not, this leads you down the path of being a big traffic getting site but with low sales)

How to Avoid:

Ensure High Conversion Rates: Utilize techniques to keep conversion rates high, still working on clear CTA (call-to-action), & bringing good offers while paying attention to landing pages which should be optimized.

Performance Tracking: Analytics tools will help you track the sources of traffic and user behavior, along with conversion rate.

6. Not Tracking and Measuring Metrics

Mistake #6: If you are not tracking and testing your KPIs, which will block your streamline process on what works best for the campaign.

How to avoid:

- Analytics Tools: Consider the likes of Google Analytical, affiliate dashboards or any other tracking software that helps you to understand where do you fall on clicks/ conversion and revenues.

Regularly: Spend some time reviewing your performance data for trends and assess their relevance so you can take action when necessary.

7. Not Optimizing for Mobile

Mistake #7: You may fail to convert mobile traffic due to bad user experience when you do not have the optimized website and content for Mobile users.

How to Avoid:

Responsive Design: Make sure website and the content are mobile friendly. Have people try your site on a number of devices for usability.

Optimizing Speed — The mobile site need to be accelerated by compressing images (as the average page load time is very high), reducing code, and hosting.

8. Spamming with Affiliate links

Mistake #8: If you overdo it with using affiliate links in a short period of time, this can easily be translated into aggressive tactics by your readers and they may become more cautious when clicking those links or converting through them.

How to avoid:

Put affiliate links strategically in your content, It should be ensured that the links are contextually related and subtle in terms of origin.

Adjust affiliate links to add a bit of value and actually recommend things people want.

9. Not Building an Email List

Mistake #9: If you do not build an email list, then the odds of your target audience responding to any calls-to-action (CTAs) and returning for repeat traffic or sales, are all going down.

How to avoid:

Email Marketing – Create an email list and keep it warmed up. Give sign up incentives like free resources or exclusive content.

- Communicate Often: Keep them in the loop via email but add context with your affiliate offers.

10. Relying on One Traffic Source

Mistake #10: Relying exclusively upon a single resource is that you are exposed to it up and down or otherwise plan & algorithm revisions.

How to Avoid:

Traffic sources of yours are organic search, social media, paid advertising and email marketing for instance. Diversification of the traffic ensures risk coverage as well expands your reach on a wider base.

Discover More Traffic Channels: There is a need to stay on top of new traffic channels and leverage them effectively whenever you can find something that drives not just new visitors but also engagement.

11. Not Doing Competitor Analysis

Mistake #11: Failing to watch the competition may leave you clueless about a unique opportunity or how some markets have shifted on strategy.

How to Avoid:

Competitive Research- Regularly monitor your competitors to benchmark what they are doing in terms of strategy, content and performance discern gaps and opportunities for differentiation.

Benchmarking: Compare where you stand and how can it be improvised using data from competitors.

12.   Failing at Testing and Optimizing

Mistake #12: Not testing and tweaking strategies, leading to underperformance but also opportunity cost.

How to Avoid:

A/B Testing: This is where you test various components of your campaign such as headlines, CTAs or landing pages - everything to learn what works best

Continuous Improvement — It currently takes the test results and performance data to improve strategies continually.

13. Not developing relationships with affiliate managers

Mistake #13: No one who earns a living is so caught up in building relationships with affiliate managers that they miss out on the opportunity and lose the assistance.

How to Avoid:

–Regular Communication: You must always keep in touch with the account managers. Seek their advice and provide feedback, keep current with new initiatives, etc.

- Partnerships: This is important due to the fact that we need those great partnerships with your affiliate managers and other affiliates so you can share insights, ask for assistance etc.

14. Setting Vague Or No Goals and Objectives

Mistake #4: Without clear goals and objectives, all your efforts can get diffused without any way of measuring what success looks like.

How to Avoid:

What are your goals: Create SMARTB Goals (specific, measurable, achievable advertising relevant time bound).

Track Progress — Monitor progress against goals and adjust strategies as needed to keep heading in the right direction.

Affiliate Marketing is the Future

Affiliate marketing has come a long way since its inception and delivers even more evolution in the future. Affiliate marketing will certainly grow and evolve in response to technological advancements, changes in consumer behavior and new trends.

1. A rise in Artificial Intelligence and Automation

– AI-Enabled Analytics: With the increased sophistication of AI being used in conjunction with other tool + information types, data analysis will continue to improve as a result providing deeper customer behaviors, campaign performances and trends. It helps in optimizing targeting, tailoring recommendations and predicting future performance with the use of advanced AI tools.

Automation: Automation will automate repetitive tasks as email marketing, ad management and reporting. Tasks that are routine in nature can be managed automatically and marketers will then focus on strategic activities.

Chatbots: As AI becomes more advanced, chatbots will be used for customer interactions and support. This can range from recommendations on products, to answering questions and pushing conversions.

2. Influencer or Micro-Influencer marketing

- Influencer Partnership: The rise in influencer marketing will continue as brands collaborate with influencers to target specific audiences Trusted voice and engagement: The more influencers are able to communicate with their followers the higher increase of trust will be.

Micro-Influencers: This could put a spotlight on micro-influencers, because those with small audiences so long as they are engaged enough will still offer value.

These genuine relationships and unique niches can significantly increase the engagement & conversion rates.

Performance-Based Compensation: Increased numbers of influencers will be paid based on performance metrics, incentivizing more to act like affiliate marketers and actually focus on conversions or sales.

3. Mobile and Voice Commerce also Widen in its Adoption

Mobile Optimization: With the rise of mobile commerce, affiliate marketers must optimize their strategies to work on mobile devices. Think mobile-friendly websites, apps and ad formats.

— Voice Search and Commerce: The rise of voice-activated devices, such as smart speakers. Success lies in being able to optimize for voice search and looking at how marketing can capitalize off of what is likely the next generation's ecommerce breakthrough.

4. Better Personalization, Customer Experience

Personalized Content — With advanced data analytics, provide personalized content and offers Personalization of recommendations to user behavior and preferences leads to better engagement and consequently higher conversions.

Customer Journey Mapping: This skill will be an indispensable component in the toolbox of any marketer, to understand and improve customer journey. Data is what will enable marketers to deliver consistent, cohesive and personalized touchpoints from initial consumer interaction until purchase.

5. Increased Transparency and Compliance Focus

Regulatory Compliance: The data privacy landscape is changing rapidly, and as laws evolve it will be even more important for affiliate marketers to avoid compliance pitfalls.

Following things like GDPR or CCPA rules is going to be critical in not only being trusted by users but also legal action.

- Transparency: A greater focus on transparency will be necessary to retain credibility. The result will be full disclosure of affiliate relationships and straight reviews.

6. Integrating with New Technologies

Blockchain Technology — Blockchain may change the game of the affiliate marketing by making transparency underground nuclear bunkers, rampant fraudulence and seamless.

Affiliate partnerships might become increasingly easier with the arrival of smart contracts and decentralized networks.

Augmented Reality (AR) and Virtual Reality (VR): Strides in AR and VR technology will benefit customers by providing them an improved shopping experience, where they can see the product actually being used on a virtual runway or have it tried-on virtually so as to give that 'real' feeling. These technologies can be incorporated into the strategies of affiliates to engage.

7. Native advertising has been supplanted by the rise of content marketing

Content Marketing, Affiliate marketers can rely more on high-quality content. Indeed, writing quality and shareable content that satisfies exceptional visitor requirements — will lead masses to you incentivizing conversions.

Native Advertising: Native ads, that vamp in with editorial content, will become more prevalent. With this strategy, your ad remains relatively unobtrusive and leads to higher performance which makes everyone happy.

8. New Market and Platform Expansion

- Global Expansion: The scope of affiliate marketing will broaden with affiliates venturing into newer international markets in the coming years. In a global campaign context, success will rely heavily on localization strategies and insight into regional preferences.

- New social media platforms and digital channels: Affiliate marketing opportunities will expand further with new emerging social media, web 3. To be able to reach new audiences, it will also become imperative that content marketers get more inventive about how they stay on top of trends and explore other platforms.

9. The state of the Market Before and After Affiliate Networks And Programs

Affiliate Networks: Affiliate networks will become more powerful in supporting affiliates through their tools and services. With improved reporting, fraud detection and performance analytics; the network will be able to function more smoothly with greater reliability.

– Better Overall Programs — Affiliate programs are becoming more complex and offering affiliates unique opportunities including a mix of flat tiered commissions, performance bonuses, & exclusive deals. Each of these programs will be a program that can not only tailored to meet differing market conditions but also strategies.

10. Social Commerce Integration

Social Media Integration: As social commerce continues to grow, expect more sales transactions through directly within the platforms. How affiliates will use social media (shoppable posts, live streams, and social proof) to drive sales.

Social Proof: The impact and relevance of user-generated content, reviews, testimonials on social media which essentially targets the audience has a major role in an affiliate marketing.

11. Focus on Data Privacy and Security

— Data Privacy: The biggest threat to affiliate marketing is the intelligence of their data that they possess while, with every passing year privacy laws are getting tighter around them. This is going to be essential in ensuring that consumer trust doesn't begin eroding, which means having iron-clad data protection measures and clear-cut privacy policies.

- Ethical Data and Marketing: Soon, the ethical use of data in collection methods and marketing strategies will be paramount. Brand reputation, and customer trust will be determined by such ethical considerations.

12. Improved Affiliates Coaching and Improvement

– Skills Development: New learning and skill development will be key success factors for affiliates going forward. With the continuing evolution in technology and trends, affiliates need training programs, workshops and certifications.

Community Building — Last but not least, join and create affiliate marketing communities to launch better networking opportunities with experienced professionals who could answer questions or even help in solving any possible paranoia will be a great experience. Collaboration + Knowledge Sharing (learn from other affiliates!) — will be useful for all the affiliates.

Other Books by The Author

 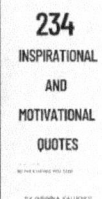 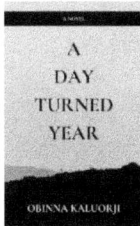 

www.ingramcontent.com/pod-product-compliance
Lightning Source LLC
Chambersburg PA
CBHW050303230526
45471CB00005B/1998